The Wicked Wit of
WOMEN

The Wicked Wit of
WOMEN

Compiled, edited and introduced by
DOMINIQUE ENRIGHT

MICHAEL O'MARA BOOKS LIMITED

First published in Great Britain in 2002 by
Michael O'Mara Books Limited
9 Lion Yard, Tremadoc Road
London sw4 7nq

Formerly published, as *Wicked, Witty and Wise: a collection
of women's witticisms from life and literature*, in 2000
by Michael O'Mara Books Limited

A CIP catalogue record for this book is available
from the British Library

isbn 1-84317-011-6

1 3 5 7 9 10 8 6 4 2

Designed and typeset by Martin Bristow

Printed and bound in Finland by WS Bookwell, Juva

Contents

Introduction

'A WOMAN'S PREACHING is like a dog's walking on his hinder legs. It is not done well: but you are surprised to find it done at all.' This comment from the great Dr Johnson, a wise man who had a number of women friends with whom he enjoyed intellectual conversation, reflects an attitude that seems to have prevailed among the compilers of most standard anthologies of quotations, where you may find at least ten quotations from men to every quotation from a woman, which *is* surprising as women have never had a reputation for saying little or nothing.

Many great novelists, for example, are women (some, indeed, admired and encouraged by Samuel Johnson) and wrote much that is quotable. But well before Johnson's time there were numerous well-established and published women writers all over the world, not to mention women who were great scholars, warriors or monarchs, just a handful of whom are quoted here. There is Hypatia – a Greek philosopher and writer of the fourth century, as well as astronomer, mathematician and head of the Neoplatonist school in Alexandria – who was murdered by Christians who objected to her scientific rationalism. From tenth-century Japan come Sei Shonagon, who served at the imperial court and whose notebooks contain a detailed account of life there, and Murasaki Shikibu, generally credited with the author-ship of *The Tale of Genji*, about the life and loves of Prince Genji.

Britain had its fair share of quotable women: the daunt-less queen of the Iceni, Boudicca, who taunted her warriors into action against the Romans: 'As for you men, you may, if you please, live and be slaves.' Or another formidable queen – Elizabeth I – who countered opposition with severity: 'I will make you shorter by the head.' There are the no-longer famous such as Susannah Centlivre (1669–1723), recog-nized by Alexander Pope, but now barely heard of, who had something pertinent to complain about – 'The carping mal-ice of the vulgar world, who think it a proof of sense to dis-like every thing that is writ by women.'

There are the women who are better known by male names – George Sand (Amandine-Aurore Lucille Dupin, Baronne Dudevant,1804–76), George Eliot (Mary Ann Evans, 1819–90), Isak Dinesen (Karen Blixen, 1885–1962), Miles Franklin (Stella Maria Sarah Miles Franklin, 1879–1954). There are women better known for fashion (Coco Chanel, Elizabeth Arden); for being on the silver screen (Hedy Lamarr, Louise Brooks, Jean Harlow), for singing (Nellie Melba), dancing (Anna Pavlova), for their depiction on screen (like the American Helen Keller, the blind and deaf child portrayed in the film, *The Miracle Worker*, later a writer and academic), or for an untimely death brought about by an accident with a scarf (Isadora Duncan).

And then there are the wives of the famous – one of Picasso's wives clearly doesn't think much of his cubic women; 'Why don't you write books people can read?' Nora Joyce complains to her husband; Catherine Blake grumbles that she never sees her husband, the visionary poet William Blake; and Mrs Gladstone is not afraid to tell the Prime Min-ister he can be pretty boring . . .

[8]

This book comprises a selection of the wisest and wittiest utterances of women from the sixth century BC right up to the 1950s; from as far east as Japan, to America, symbol of the West. There are wise words on life or love, wicked remarks about friends or public figures, witty comments on politics or society . . . Other than a tendency to emphasize the non-superiority of men – 'Even his ignorance is of a sounder quality,' George Eliot remarks ironically of the male of the species; and the odd remark that a man might consider 'bitchy', such as Barbara Stanwyck's opinion of a rising film star: 'Her body has gone to her head' – there is little that points to the quotations coming from women. As the American writer Charlotte Perkins Gilman, pointed out, 'There is no female mind. The brain is not an organ of sex. As well speak of a female liver.'

No Matter What Fork You Use

Manners and Meals

Civility costs nothing and buys everything.
LADY MARY WORTLEY MONTAGU
(1689–1762)

☽♬♬☾

Incessant company is as bad as solitary confinement.
VIRGINIA WOOLF (1882–1941)

☽♬♬☾

Superior people never make long visits.
MARIANNE MOORE (1887–1972), 1935

☽♬♬☾

I do not want people to be very agreeable as it saves me
the trouble of liking them a great deal.
JANE AUSTEN (1775–1817)

☽♬♬☾

Minute attention to propriety stops the growth of virtue.
MARY WOLLSTONECRAFT GODWIN
(1759–97)

☽♬♬☾

It is bad *ton* to overwhelm with insipid flattery all
women that we meet, without distinction of age, rank or
merit. It may indeed please some of light and frivolous
minds, but will disgust a woman of good sense.
MADAME CELNART (1796–1865)

The tragedy of English cooking is that 'plain' cooking cannot be entrusted to 'plain' cooks.

COUNTESS MORPHY (Marcelle Azra Forbes), 1935

꒰ꔛꔘꔚ꒱

Tact is after all a kind of mind-reading.

SARAH ORNE JEWETT (1849–1909)

꒰ꔛꔘꔚ꒱

Nothing is so delicate as the reputation of a woman; it is at once the most beautiful and most brittle of all human things.

JANE WELSH CARLYLE (1801–66)

Good taste is the worst vice ever invented.

EDITH SITWELL (1887–1964)

ʒʀʀʒ

Until you've lost your reputation, you never realize what a burden it was or what freedom really is.

MARGARET MITCHELL (1900–49)

ʒʀʀʒ

Manners are a sensitive awareness of the feelings of others. If you have that awareness, you have good manners, no matter what fork you use.

EMILY POST (1873–1960)

We invite people like that to tea, but we don't marry them.

LADY CHETWODE, of her son-in-law-to-be
John Betjeman, 1932

I rang for ice, but *this* is ridiculous.

MADELINE TALMAGE ASTOR (? –1945)
as she was being helped over the rail of the *Titanic*,
April 1912

჻

The English never smash in a face. They merely refrain
from asking it to dinner.

MARGARET HALSEY (1910–97), 1938

჻

There's nothing on earth to do here but look at the view
and eat. You can imagine the result since I do not like to
look at views.

ZELDA FITZGERALD (1900–48)

The Desire to Tell a Good Story

Tittle-Tattle and Lies

There is no such thing as conversation. It is an illusion.
There are intersecting monologues, that is all.

REBECCA WEST (1892–1983), 1935

❧

Blessed is the man who, having nothing to say, abstains
from giving in words evidence of the fact.

GEORGE ELIOT (Mary Ann Evans, 1819–90)

❧

Rumour never delays.

HROSWITHA OF GANDERSHEIM
(*c.* 935–1000)

❧

Have you heard of the terrible family They,
And the dreadful, venomous things They say?
Why, half of the gossip under the sun,
If you trace it back, you will find begun
In that wretched House of They.

ELLA WHEELER WILCOX
(1855–1919)

❧

Report is mightily given to magnify.

FANNY BURNEY
(Frances, Madame d'Arblay, 1752–1840)

Bette and I are very good friends. There's nothing I
wouldn't say to her face – both of them.

> TALLULAH BANKHEAD (1903–68) on Bette Davis,
> after filming *All About Eve* (released 1950)
> in which they co-starred

🌀🐾

. . . in few people is discretion stronger than the desire
to tell a good story.

> MURASAKI SHIKIBU (974–?1031)

🌀🐾

She tells enough white lies to ice a wedding cake.

> MARGOT ASQUITH (Countess of Oxford and Asquith,
> 1864–1945) of Lady Desborough

🌀🐾

His very frankness is a falsity. In fact, it seems falser than
his insincerity.

> KATHERINE MANSFIELD (1888–1923) on her husband
> John Middleton Murry

🌀🐾

At a party in Hollywood:

JEAN HARLOW: Why, you are Margo*tt* Asquith, aren't
  you?
LADY ASQUITH: No, my dear. I am Margot Asquith.
  The 't' is silent, as in Harlow.

Nobody is such a fool as to moider away his time in the slipslop conversation of a pack of women.

LADY HESTER STANHOPE (1776–1839)

⌇ℛℛ⌇

When anger spreads through the breast, guard thy tongue from barking idly.

SAPPHO (7th–6th century BC)

⌇ℛℛ⌇

If you do not tell the truth about yourself you cannot tell it about other people.

VIRGINIA WOOLF (1882–1941)

⌇ℛℛ⌇

Nobody speaks the truth when there's something they must have.

ELIZABETH BOWEN (1899–1973), 1935

⌇ℛℛ⌇

If it's very painful for you to criticize your friends – you're safe in doing it. But if you take the slightest pleasure in it – that's the time to hold your tongue.

ALICE DUER MILLER (1874–1942)

⌇ℛℛ⌇

On every formal visit a child ought to be of the party by way of provision for discourse.

JANE AUSTEN (1775–1817)

I'll not listen to reason. Reason always means what someone else has got to say.

Elizabeth Gaskell (1810–65)

ᔕᖇᖇᙅ

To-day I pronunced a word which should never come
out of a lady's lips it was that I called John a Impudent
Bitch.

Marjory Fleming (1803–11)

Don't Do It in the Street and Frighten the Horses

It doesn't matter what you do in the bedroom as long as you don't do it in the street and frighten the horses.

Mrs Patrick (Beatrice Stella) Campbell
(1865–1940)

჻ꙮꙮ჻

If all the girls attending it were laid end to end . . . I wouldn't be at all surprised.

Dorothy Parker (1893–1967),
referring to the Yale Prom, 1934 (attr.)

჻ꙮꙮ჻

Wit in women is apt to have bad consequences; like a sword without a scabbard, it wounds the wearer and provokes assailants. I am sorry to say the generality of women who have excelled in wit have failed in chastity.

Elizabeth Montagu (1720–1800)

჻ꙮꙮ჻

When a man seduces a woman, it should, I think, be termed a left-handed marriage.

Mary Wollstonecraft Godwin
(1759–97)

჻ꙮꙮ჻

There are no more thorough prudes than those who have some little secret to hide.

George Sand (Amandine-Aurore Lucille Dupin,
Baronne Dudevant, 1804–76)

Ducking for apples – change one letter and it's the story
of my life.

Dorothy Parker (1893–1967)

ᘓᕷᕷᘓ

All my lovers have been geniuses; it's the one thing on
which I insist.

Isadora Duncan (1878–1927)

ᘓᕷᕷᘓ

Brevity is the soul of lingerie, as the Petticoat said to the
Chemise.

Dorothy Parker (1893–1967), 1916

ᘓᕷᕷᘓ

The worst sin – perhaps the only sin – passion can
commit, is to be joyless.

Dorothy L. Sayers (1893–1957), 1936

Love ceases to be a pleasure when it ceases to be a secret.

APHRA BEHN (1640–89)

⌇⌇⌇

I have heard much of these languishing lovers, but I never yet saw one of them die for love.

MARGARET OF NAVARRE (Marguerite d'Angoulême,
Queen of Navarre, 1492–1549)

⌇⌇⌇

> It is well within the order of things
> That man should listen when his mate sings;
> But the true male never yet walked
> Who liked to listen when his mate talked.

ANNA WICKHAM (1884–1947)

⌇⌇⌇

Scratch a lover and find a foe.

DOROTHY PARKER (1893–1967), 1937

Smoke into Gold

Money

I must say I hate money but it's the lack of it I hate most.

KATHERINE MANSFIELD (1888–1923)

ɜɷɛ

Come away; poverty's catching.

APHRA BEHN (1640–89)

ɜɷɛ

There are people who have money and people who are rich.

COCO CHANEL (Gabrielle Bonheur, 1883–1971)

Adversity is solitary, while prosperity dwells in a crowd.

Marguerite de Valois (1553–1615)

༄༅༈

Prosperity seldom chooses the side of the virtuous.

Héloïse (1098–1164)

༄༅༈

I have known many people who turned their gold into smoke, but you are the first to turn smoke into gold.

Elizabeth I (1533–1603) to Sir Walter Ralegh

༄༅༈

. . . money demoralizes even the giver.

Marceline Desbordes-Valmore (1786–1859)

༄༅༈

Nothing melts a woman's heart like gold.

Susannah Centlivre (c. 1669–1723)

Leave off the agony, leave off style,
Unless you've got money by you all the while.
JULIA A. MOORE (1847–1920)

〜〜〜

If we had no winter, the spring would not be so
pleasant; if we did not sometimes taste of adversity,
prosperity would not be so welcome.
ANNE BRADSTREET (*c.* 1612–72)

〜〜〜

I was mad about clothes for a time. You know, ermine
coats and those things eat up a lot of money.
LOUISE BROOKS (1906–85)

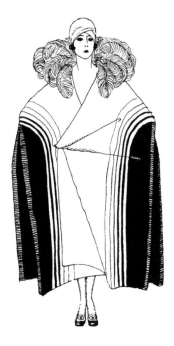

A Yankee (I speak of the common-minded) calculates
his generosity and sympathy as methodically as his
income; and to waste either, on an unprofitable, or
undeserving, object would be foolish, if not wicked.

SARAH JOSEPHA HALE (1788–1879)

꒱ꪀꪀꪑ

. . . he had never heard Americans conversing without
the word 'DOLLAR' being pronounced between them.

FRANCES TROLLOPE (1780–1863)

꒱ꪀꪀꪑ

A large income is the best recipe for happiness I ever
heard of. It certainly may secure all the myrtle and
turkey part of it.

JANE AUSTEN (1775–1817)

꒱ꪀꪀꪑ

Poverty? Wealth? Seek neither –
One causes swollen heads,
The other, swollen bellies.

KASSIA (9th century AD)

꒱ꪀꪀꪑ

I do want to get rich but I never want to do what there is
to do to get rich.

GERTRUDE STEIN (1874–1946);
Miss Stein was herself quite rich

The longer I live, the more I grow in the opinion that it is useless to pile up wealth.

Françoise d'Aubigné, Madame de Maintenon
(1635–1719), governess to Louis XIV's children;
she married him after the queen's death

⟆⟆⟆

Business is other people's money.

Delphine de Girardin (1804–55)

⟆⟆⟆

Money alone determines your entire life, political as well as private.

Germaine Necker, Madame de Staël
(1766–1817)

⟆⟆⟆

People don't resent having nothing nearly as much as too little.

Ivy Compton-Burnett (1884–1969), 1939

A High Altar
on the Move

Appearance

The perpetual hunger to be beautiful and that thirst to be loved which is the real curse of Eve.

JEAN RHYS (*c.* 1890–1979), 1927

ろりりろ

Nature gives you the face you have at twenty; it is up to you to merit the face you have at fifty.

COCO CHANEL (Gabrielle Bonheur, 1883–1971)

ろりりろ

A high altar on the move.

ELIZABETH BOWEN (1899–1973)
on Edith Sitwell's appearance

ろりりろ

'You look rather rash my dear your colors dont quite match your face.'

DAISY ASHFORD (1881–1972)

A dirty exterior is a great enemy to beauty of all descriptions.

MARY MARTHA SHERWOOD (1775–1851)

🙰

Vanity, like murder, will out.

HANNAH COWLEY (1743–1809)

🙰

This Englishwoman is so refined
She has no bosom and no behind.

STEVIE SMITH
(1902–71), 1937

🙰

As she had no hope of raising herself to the rank of a beauty, her only chance was bringing others down to her own level.

EMILY EDEN (1797–1869)

The sense of being well-dressed gives a feeling of inward tranquillity which religion is powerless to bestow.

MISS C. F. FORBES (1817–1911)

᠄᠄᠄

Her body has gone to her head.

BARBARA STANWYCK (1907–90)
on a rising film star

᠄᠄᠄

Where's the man could ease a heart
Like a satin gown?

DOROTHY PARKER (1893–1967), 1927

᠄᠄᠄

To write, to read, or think, or to enquire
Would cloud our beauty . . .

ANNE FINCH (1661– *c.* 1722)

᠄᠄᠄

Happiness is in your power, though beauty is not; and on that to set too high a value would be pardonable only in a weak and frivolous mind.

FANNY BURNEY (Frances,
Madame d'Arblay, 1752–1840)

᠄᠄᠄

Beauty endures for only as long as it can be seen; goodness, beautiful today, will remain so tomorrow.

SAPPHO (7th–6th century BC)

[36]

I had always looked upon my beauty as a curse, because
I was regarded as a whore, rather than an actress. Now
at least I understand that my beauty was a blessing. It
was my lack of understanding the way to merchandise it
that was the curse.

LOUISE BROOKS (1906–85)

🙛🙙

When a woman looks at a man in evening dress, she
sometimes can't help wondering why he wants to blazon
his ancestry to the world by wearing a coat with a long
tail to it.

HELEN ROWLAND (1875–1950)

If it were the fashion to go naked, the face would be
hardly observed.

LADY MARY WORTLEY MONTAGU
(1689–1762)

⳥ⱤⱤⳣ

'Good heavens!' said he, 'if it be our clothes alone which
fit us for society, how highly we should esteem those who
make them.'

MARIE VON EBNER-ESCHENBACH
(1830–1916)

⳥ⱤⱤⳣ

Man is of a dull, earthy, and melancholy aspect, having
fallowes in his face, and a very forrest upon his chin,
when our soft and smooth cheeks are a true representa-
tion of a delectable garden of intermixed roses and
lilies.

MARY TATTLEWELL (*fl.*1640)

It is now eleven years since I have seen my figure in a glass, and the last reflection I saw there was so disagreeable, that I resolved to spare myself the mortification in the future.

LADY MARY WORTLEY MONTAGU
(1689–1762)

૩ᏕᏕ

I would gladly give half of the wit with which I am credited for half of the beauty you possess.

Germaine Necker, MADAME DE STAËL
(1766–1817) to Juliette Récamier

૩ᏕᏕ

There were very few beauties, and such as there were were not very handsome . . . Mrs Blount was the only one much admired. She appeared exactly as she did in September, with the same broad face, diamond bandeau, white shoes, pink husband, and fat neck.

JANE AUSTEN (1775–1817)

It is hardly surprising that women concentrate on the way they look instead of what is in their minds since not much has been put in their minds to begin with.

MARY SHELLEY (1797–1851)

ℭ

Beauty with all the helps of Art, is of no long date; the more it is help'd, the sooner it decays.

MARY ASTELL (1668–1731)

To me Edith looks like something that would eat its young.

Dorothy Parker (1893–1967) on Dame Edith Evans

ϽᏜᏜԋ

Any girl can be glamorous. All you have to do is stand still and look stupid.

Hedy Lamarr (1914–2000)

ϽᏜᏜԋ

A homely face and no figure have aided many women heavenward.

Minna Antrim (1861–1950)

Such a Nice Change

Age

Exchange in a doorway:
CLARE BOOTHE LUCE, *stepping aside:* Age before beauty.
DOROTHY PARKER, *sweeping through:* Pearls before swine.

꒷ꆚꆚ꒽

> But the fruit that can fall without shaking
> Indeed is too mellow for me.
> > LADY MARY WORTLEY MONTAGU (1689–1762)

꒷ꆚꆚ꒽

The years that a woman subtracts from her age are not
lost. They are added to the ages of other women.
> DIANE DE POITIERS (1499–1566)

꒷ꆚꆚ꒽

We grow old as soon as we cease to love and trust.
> LOUISE-HONORÉ DE CHOISEUL (1734–1801)

꒷ꆚꆚ꒽

I'm not interested in age. People who tell me their age
are silly. You're as old as you feel.
> ELIZABETH ARDEN *(c.* 1880–1966)

꒷ꆚꆚ꒽

One of the signs of passing youth is the birth of a sense
of fellowship with other human beings as we take our
place among them.
> VIRGINIA WOOLF (1882–1941)

One of the many things nobody ever tells you about middle age is that it's such a nice change from being young.

DOROTHY CANFIELD FISHER (1879–1958)

🐱🐾🐾🐱

We grow neither better nor worse as we get old, but more like ourselves.

MAY LAMBERTON BECKER (1873–1958)

🐱🐾🐾🐱

One keeps forgetting old age up to the very brink of the grave.

(Sidonie-Gabrielle) COLETTE (1873–1954)

🐱🐾🐾🐱

We are always the same age inside.

GERTRUDE STEIN (1874–1946)

🐱🐾🐾🐱

In youth we learn; in age we understand.

MARIE VON EBNER-ESCHENBACH (1830–1916)

Youth is the time of getting, middle age of improving,
and old age of spending.

ANNE BRADSTREET (*c.* 1612–72)

🦚🦚

If youth is the season of hope, it is often so only in the
sense that our elders are hopeful about us.

GEORGE ELIOT (Mary Ann Evans, 1819–90)

🦚🦚

A woman has the age she deserves.

COCO CHANEL (Gabrielle Bonheur, 1883–1971)

🦚🦚

When a noble life has prepared for old age, it is not
decline that it reveals, but the first days of immortality.

Germaine Necker, MADAME DE STAËL
(1766–1817)

🦚🦚

It is so comic to hear oneself called old, even at ninety I
suppose!

ALICE JAMES (1848–92)

🦚🦚

Eyes of youth have sharp sight, but commonly not so
deep as those of elder age.

ELIZABETH I (1533–1603)

I refuse to admit that I am more than fifty-two, even if
that does make my sons illegitimate.

NANCY, LADY ASTOR (1879–1964)

ᏬᏖᏖᏬ

We grow old more through indolence, than through
age.

CHRISTINA, QUEEN OF SWEDEN
(1626–89)

ᏬᏖᏖᏬ

Surely the consolation prize of age is in finding out how
few things are worth worrying over, and how many
things that we once desired, we don't want any more.

DOROTHY DIX (1861–1951)

You can stay young as long as you can learn, acquire new habits and suffer contradiction.

MARIE VON EBNER-ESCHENBACH (1830–1916)

ᔕᕈᕪᔓ

Very young people are true but not resounding instruments.

ELIZABETH BOWEN (1899–1973), 1938

ᔕᕈᕪᔓ

We are tomorrow's past.

MARY WEBB (1881–1927)

A Sincere Interest

Politics and Politicians

I have changed my ministers, but I have not changed my measures. I am still for moderation and will govern by it.

QUEEN ANNE (1665–1714)
to a new Tory ministry

꒰ঌ♠❤꒱

Congress . . . these – for the most part – illiterate hacks whose fancy vests are spotted with gravy and whose speeches, hypocritical, unctuous and slovenly, are spotted also with the gravy of political patronage.

MARY MCCARTHY (1912–89), 1946

꒰ঌ♠❤꒱

Proud Prelate, you know what you were before I made you what you are now. If you do not comply with my request, I will unfrock you, by God.

ELIZABETH I (1533–1603)
to Dr Richard Cox

꒰ঌ♠❤꒱

An election is coming. Universal peace is declared, and the foxes have a sincere interest in prolonging the lives of the poultry.

GEORGE ELIOT
(Mary Ann Evans, 1819–90)

꒰ঌ♠❤꒱

Political controversies are never entered into with any wish to gain knowledge, but only a triumph for the party.

SARAH JOSEPHA HALE (1788–1879)

Never lose your temper with the Press or the public is a major rule of political life.

CHRISTABEL PANKHURST (1880–1958)

❧

The argument of the broken window pane is the most valuable argument in modern politics.

EMMELINE PANKHURST (1858–1928)

❧

Freedom is always and exclusively freedom for the one who thinks differently.

ROSA LUXEMBURG (1871–1919)

❧

O liberty! O liberty! What crimes are committed in thy name.

JEANNE-MARIE, MADAME ROLAND (1754–93);
her last official words before being guillotined
for opposing Robespierre and Danton

❧

A society in which consumption has to be artificially stimulated in order to keep production going is a society founded on trash and waste, and such a society is a house built on sand.

DOROTHY L. SAYERS (1893–1957), 1947

If American politics are too dirty for women to take part
in, there's something wrong with American politics.
ᴇᴅɴᴀ ꜰᴇʀʙᴇʀ (1887–1968)

※

I shall be an autocrat: that's my trade. And the good
Lord will forgive me: that's his.
ᴄᴀᴛʜᴇʀɪɴᴇ ᴛʜᴇ ɢʀᴇᴀᴛ, Empress of Russia
(1729–96)

※

. . . arbitrary power is, like most other things that are
very hard, very liable to be broken.
ᴀʙɪɢᴀɪʟ ᴀᴅᴀᴍꜱ (1744–1888)

※

I will make you shorter by the head.
ᴇʟɪᴢᴀʙᴇᴛʜ ɪ (1533–1603) to the leaders of her Council
when they opposed her policy on Mary, Queen of Scots

※

History is busy with us.
ᴍᴀʀɪᴇ-ᴀɴᴛᴏɪɴᴇᴛᴛᴇ, Queen Consort of France
(Josèphe Jeanne Marie-Antoinette, 1755–93)
at the revolutionary tribunal

※

Authority without wisdom is like a heavy axe without an
edge, fitter to bruise than polish.
ᴀɴɴᴇ ʙʀᴀᴅꜱᴛʀᴇᴇᴛ (c. 1612–72)

Lying is an occupation
Used by all who mean to rise;
Politicians owe their station
But to well-concerted lies.

LAETITIA PILKINGTON (1712–50)

༄༅༄

The pursuit of politics is religion, morality, and poetry
all in one.

Germaine Necker, MADAME DE STAËL
(1766–1817)

༄༅༄

The female chest was not made for hanging orders on.

'GENEVIÈVE', 1850

༄༅༄

No influence so quickly converts a radical into a
reactionary as does his election to power.

ELISABETH MARBURY (1856–1933)

༄༅༄

Morality must guide calculation, and calculation must
guide politics.

Germaine Necker, MADAME DE STAËL
(1766–1817)

༄༅༄

But politics poison the mind.

MARCELINE DESBORDES-VALMORE (1786–1859)

Well, I've got you the presidency – what are you going to do with it?

FLORENCE HARDING (1860–1924) to her husband,
US President Warren G. Harding

જ્ઞબર

Well, Mr Baldwin, *this* is a pretty kettle of fish!

QUEEN MARY (1867–1953) to the Prime Minister,
on the abdication of her son, Edward VIII, 1936

જ્ઞબર

From politics, it was an easy step to silence.

JANE AUSTEN (1775–1817)

He speaks to Me as if I was a public meeting.

QUEEN VICTORIA (1819–1901)
on William Ewart Gladstone

ᘔ᙮᙮ᘔ

If you weren't such a great man you'd be a terrible bore.

MRS WILLIAM GLADSTONE
to her husband William Ewart Gladstone

ᘔ᙮᙮ᘔ

. . . two-thirds mush and one-third Eleanor [his wife].

ALICE ROOSEVELT LONGWORTH (1884–1980)
on her distant cousin, US President Franklin D. Roosevelt

ᘔ᙮᙮ᘔ

He has a brilliant mind until he makes it up.

MARGOT ASQUITH (Countess of Oxford and Asquith,
1864–1945) on Sir Stafford Cripps

ᘔ᙮᙮ᘔ

He looks as if he had been weaned on a pickle.

ALICE ROOSEVELT LONGWORTH (1884–1980)
on US President Calvin Coolidge

ᘔ᙮᙮ᘔ

How can they tell?

DOROTHY PARKER (1893–1967) on hearing
that US President Calvin Coolidge was dead, 1933

He's very clever, but sometimes his brains go to his head.

MARGOT ASQUITH (Countess of Oxford and Asquith, 1864–1945) of F. E. Smith

༄༅༅༄

He could not see a belt without hitting below it.

MARGOT ASQUITH (Countess of Oxford and Asquith, 1864–1945) on David Lloyd George

༄༅༅༄

Thomas Dewey is just about the nastiest little man I've ever known. He struts sitting down.

MRS CLARENCE DYKSTRA of the American politician Thomas E. Dewey

༄༅༅༄

He would kill his own mother just so that he could use her skin to make a drum to beat his own praises.

MARGOT ASQUITH (Countess of Oxford and Asquith, 1864–1945) on Winston Churchill

That Kind
of Patriotism

War and Peace

That kind of patriotism which consists in hating all
other nations.

ELIZABETH GASKELL (1810–65)

ᔕᗡᗢᓂ

Before a war military science seems a real science, like
astronomy; but after a war, it seems more like astrology.

REBECCA WEST (1892–1983)

ᔕᗡᗢᓂ

The heresy of one age becomes the orthodoxy of the
next.

HELEN KELLER (1880–1968)

ᔕᗡᗢᓂ

Providence is always on the side of the big battalions.

Marie de Rabutin-Chantal, MADAME DE SÉVIGNÉ
(1626–96)

ᔕᗡᗢᓂ

It is better to die on your feet than to live on your
knees.

DOLORES IBARRURI, 'LA PASIONARIA'
(1895–1989), 1936

ᔕᗡᗢᓂ

Mankind is not disposed to look narrowly into the
conduct of great victors when their victory is on the
right side.

GEORGE ELIOT (Mary Ann Evans, 1819–90)

They have not wanted *peace* at all; they have wanted to be spared war – as though the absence of war was the same as peace.

DOROTHY THOMPSON (1894–1961)

ɜ⌇ʀↄ

Monarchs ought to put to death the authors and instigators of war, as their own enemies and as dangers to their states.

ELIZABETH I (1533–1603)

ɜ⌇ʀↄ

Every political good carried to the extreme must be productive of evil.

MARY WOLLSTONECRAFT GODWIN (1759–97)

ɜ⌇ʀↄ

I do not want the peace which passeth understanding, I want the understanding which bringeth peace.

HELEN KELLER (1880–1968)

We are not interested in the possibilities of defeat; they do not exist.

QUEEN VICTORIA (1819–1901)

⟡⟡⟡

Kansas had better stop raising corn and begin raising hell.

MARY ELIZABETH LEASE (1853–1933)

⟡⟡⟡

Standing as I do, in view of God and eternity, I realize that patriotism is not enough. I must have no hatred or bitterness towards anyone.

EDITH CAVELL (1865–1915), just before her execution by the Germans on trumped-up charges of spying

⟡⟡⟡

Pray, good people, be civil. I am the Protestant whore.

NELL GWYNNE (c. 1650–87), when, during the Popish Terror of 1681, her coach was surrounded by an angry anti-Catholic mob under the impression she was another of Charles II's mistresses, Louise de Kéroualle, 'the Catholic whore', whom the King made Duchess of Portsmouth

⟡⟡⟡

People who talk about peace are very often the most quarrelsome.

NANCY, LADY ASTOR (1879–1964)

Space Where Nobody Is

Places

It is not in the temper of the people either to give or to receive.

FRANCES TROLLOPE (1780–1863) on the Americans

ʒᗡᗞꙅ

Canada is useful only to provide me with furs.

Jeanne Antoinette Poisson,
MADAME DE POMPADOUR (1721–64)

In the United States there is more space where nobody is than where anybody is. That is what makes America what it is.

GERTRUDE STEIN (1874–1946)

ʒᗡᗞꙅ

The United States is . . . a warning rather than an example to the world.

LYDIA MARIA CHILD (1802–1880)

ʒᗡᗞꙅ

America is my country and Paris is my home town.

GERTRUDE STEIN (1874–1946)

What a pity, when Christopher Columbus discovered
America, that he ever mentioned it.

MARGOT ASQUITH
(Countess of Oxford and Asquith,
1864–1945)

🙰

One has no great hopes from Birmingham. I always say
there is something direful in the sound.

JANE AUSTEN (1775–1817)

🙰

New York . . . that unnatural city where everyone is an
exile, none more so than the American.

CHARLOTTE PERKINS GILMAN (1860–1935)

There is small danger of being starved in our land of plenty [America]; but the danger of being stuffed is imminent.

SARAH JOSEPHA HALE (1788–1879)

I am American bred.
I have seen much to hate here – much to forgive,
But in a world where England is finished and dead,
I do not wish to live.

ALICE DUER MILLER (1874–1942)

The Pursuit of Culture

The Arts

So you're going to Australia! I made twenty thousand pounds on my tour there, but of course *that* will never be done again . . . All I can say is – sing 'em muck! It's all they can understand!

DAME NELLIE MELBA (1861–1931)
to Dame Clara Butt

❧ ❧

If my husband were ever to meet a woman on the street who looked like the women in his paintings, he would fall over in a dead faint.

MRS PABLO PICASSO of the famous painter

❧ ❧

I would rather be a brilliant memory than a curiosity.

EMMA EAMES (1865–1982), opera singer,
on her early retirement at the age of forty-seven

If art does not enlarge men's sympathies, it does nothing morally.

GEORGE ELIOT (Mary Ann Evans, 1819–90)

꒰꒱꒰꒱

An unalterable and unquestioned law of the musical world required that the German text of French operas sung by Swedish artists should be translated into Italian for the clearer understanding of English-speaking audiences.

EDITH WHARTON (1862–1937)

꒰꒱꒰꒱

Music is not written in red, white and blue. It is written in the heart's blood of the composer.

DAME NELLIE MELBA (1861–1931)

꒰꒱꒰꒱

If I didn't start painting, I would have raised chickens.

GRANDMA MOSES (1860–1961)

Señor Dalí, born delirious
Considers it folly to be serious.
PHYLLIS McGINLEY (1905–78)

༄༅༅༄

Oh, well, you play Bach *your* way. I'll play him his.
WANDA LANDOWSKA (1877–1959), attr.

There is less in this than meets the eye.
TALLULAH BANKHEAD (1903–68),
remark to Alexander Woollcott of a performance
of Maeterlink's *Aglavaine and Sélysette*, 1922

You ask my opinion about taking the young Salzburg musician into your service. I do not know where you can place him, since I feel you do not require a composer, or other useless people.

MARIA THERESA, EMPRESS OF AUSTRIA (1717–80),
to her son Archduke Ferdinand of Austria,
about the sixteen-year-old Mozart

☙❦❧

It's beige! My colour!

ELSIE DEWOLFE (1865–1950)
on first seeing the Acropolis

☙❦❧

Mr Lewis's pictures appeared to have been painted by a mailed fist in a cotton glove.

EDITH SITWELL (1887–1964)
on Wyndham Lewis

☙❦❧

Mrs Ballinger is one of those ladies who pursue Culture in bands, as though it were dangerous to meet it alone.

EDITH WHARTON (1862–1937)

☙❦❧

Of all the bulls that live, this hath the greatest ass's ears.

ELIZABETH I (1533–1603)
on John Bull, musician and composer

Another unsettling element in modern art is that common symptom of immaturity, the dread of doing what has been done before.

EDITH WHARTON (1862–1937)

༄༅༈

Any man who has money may obtain the reputation of taste by the mere purchasing of the works of art.

SARAH JOSEPHA HALE (1788–1879)

༄༅༈

For painters, poets and builders have very high flights, but they must be kept down.

SARAH, DUCHESS OF MARLBOROUGH (1660–1744)

Be Sparing
of Your Prose

Writers and
Their Work

No entertainment is so cheap as reading, nor any
pleasure so lasting.

LADY MARY WORTLEY MONTAGU

(1689–1762)

ᔡᘓᘖᓭ

One may lie to oneself, lie to the world, lie to God even,
but to one's pen one cannot lie.

WILLA CATHER (1873–1947)

ᔡᘓᘖᓭ

I suppose I'm a born novelist, for the things I imagine
are more vital and vivid to me than the things I
remember.

ELLEN GLASGOW (1873–1945)

ᔡᘓᘖᓭ

We again repeat that we will not accept any stories
where runaway horses or upsetting of boats is necessary
to the denouement.

SARAH JOSEPHA HALE (1788–1879)

ᔡᘓᘖᓭ

Correct English is the slang of prigs who write history
and essays. And the strongest slang of all is the slang of
poets.

GEORGE ELIOT

(Mary Ann Evans, 1819–90)

It was a book to kill time for those who like it better
dead.

ROSE MACAULAY (1889–1958)

ᘗᔑᔑᘓ

This is not a novel to be tossed aside lightly. It should be
thrown with great force.

DOROTHY PARKER (1893–1967) on the romance
Claudia Particella, l'Amante del Cardinale: Grande Romanzo dei
Tempi del Cardinal Emanuel Madruzzo . . . by Benito Mussolini

Novelists should never allow themselves to weary of the
study of real life.

CHARLOTTE BRONTË (1816–55)

ᘗᔑᔑᘓ

If I read a book that impresses me, I have to take myself
firmly in hand before I mix with other people;
otherwise they would think my mind rather queer.

ANNE FRANK (1929–45)

All autobiographies are alibi-ographies.

CLARE BOOTHE LUCE (1903–87)

❧❧❧

A woman must have money and a room of her own if she is to write fiction.

VIRGINIA WOOLF (1882–1941)

❧❧❧

Satire should, like a polished razor keen,
Wound with a touch that's scarcely felt or seen.

LADY MARY WORTLEY MONTAGU
(1689–1762)

❧❧❧

But 'twill appear, in spite of all editing,
A woman's way to charm is not by writing.

ANNE FINCH (1661– *c.* 1722)

Your poetry is bad enough, so pray be sparing of your prose.

ELIZABETH, LADY HOLLAND (1771–1845)
to the poet Samuel Rogers

꒰ꙥꙥ꒱

Virginia Woolf's writing is no more than glamorous knitting. I believe she must have a pattern somewhere.

EDITH SITWELL (1887–1964)

꒰ꙥꙥ꒱

That old Yahoo George Moore . . . His stories impressed me as being on the whole like gruel spooned up off a dirty floor.

JANE BARLOW (1860–1917)

Very Tiresome Things: When a poem of one's own, that one has allowed someone else to use as his, is singled out for praise.

SEI SHONAGON (966/7–1013?)

༄༅

The stupid person's idea of the clever person.

ELIZABETH BOWEN (1899–1973) on Aldous Huxley, 1936

༄༅

He seems to me the most vulgar-minded genius that ever produced a great effect in literature.

GEORGE ELIOT (Mary Ann Evans, 1819–90) on Lord Byron

༄༅

I am sorry to hear you are going to publish a poem. Can't you suppress it?

ELIZABETH, LADY HOLLAND (1771–1845)
to Lord Porchester

Besides Shakespeare and me, who do you think there is?

GERTRUDE STEIN (1874–1946)

🙰

He gets at the substance of a book directly; he tears out the heart of it.

MARY KNOWLES (1733–1807) on Samuel Johnson

🙰

Indeed, the freedom with which Dr Johnson condemns whatever he disapproves is astonishing.

JANE WELSH CARLYLE (1801–66)

🙰

He and I should not in the least agree of course, in our ideas of novels and heroines; – pictures of perfection as you know make me sick and wicked.

JANE AUSTEN (1775–1817) in a letter to her niece,
Fanny Knight, referring to Fanny's erstwhile suitor,
James Wildman. Fanny had lent him her aunt's
novels, which he did not like

Then why didn't you bring him with you? I should be
delighted to meet him.

EMERALD, LADY CUNARD to Somerset Maugham
when he said he was leaving some social occasion
'to keep his youth'

ᘓᕧᕧᘒ

The Doctor has a transcendental gift, when he is writing
sense, for making this appear to be nonsense . . .

EDITH SITWELL (1887–1964) of F. R. Leavis, 1934

ᘓᕧᕧᘒ

The affair between Margot Asquith and Margot Asquith
will live as one of the prettiest love stories in all literature.

DOROTHY PARKER (1893–1967) on Margot Asquith's
four-volume autobiography

ᘓᕧᕧᘒ

Why don't you write books people can read?

NORA JOYCE (1884–1965) to her husband, James Joyce

What a sense of superiority it gives one to escape
reading some book which everyone else is reading.
ALICE JAMES (1848–92) – perhaps thinking of her brother
Henry James's novels?

🙙🙚

Oh, really? What is she reading?
DAME EDITH EVANS (1888–76) when told that Nancy Mitford
had borrowed a friend's villa in order to finish a book

🙙🙚

His ignorance was an Empire State Building of ignorance.
You had to admire it for its size.
DOROTHY PARKER (1893–1967) on the editor
of the *New Yorker*, Harold Ross

🙙🙚

I don't care for Osbert's prose; the rhododendrons
grow to such a height in it.
VIRGINIA WOOLF (1882–1941)
on Osbert Sitwell

When you were a little boy, someone ought to have said
'Hush' just once.

MRS PATRICK (Beatrice Stella) CAMPBELL
(1865–1940) to George Bernard Shaw

ༀ

Mamma says that she was then the prettiest, silliest, most
affected husband-hunting butterfly she ever remembers.

MARY RUSSELL MITFORD (1787–1855)
on Jane Austen, 1815

ༀ

I think I may boast myself to be, with all possible vanity,
the most unlearned and uninformed female who ever
dared be an authoress.

JANE AUSTEN (1775–1817)

ༀ

A list of our authors who have made themselves most
beloved, and therefore most comfortable financially,
shows that it is our national joy to mistake for the first-
rate the fecund rate.

DOROTHY PARKER (1893–1967)

The old maid among novelists.

REBECCA WEST (1892–1983) on H.G. Wells . . .
with whom she had a ten-year love affair

The carping malice of the vulgar world, who think it a
proof of sense to dislike every thing that is writ by
women.

SUSANNAH CENTLIVRE (*c.* 1669–1723)

A dirty man with opium-glazed eyes and rat-taily hair.

LADY FREDERICK CAVENDISH
on Alfred, Lord Tennyson

I wish her characters would talk a little less like the
heroes and heroines of police reports.

GEORGE ELIOT (Mary Ann Evans, 1819–90)
on Charlotte Brontë

᠄᠉᠈᠉

Perpendicular, precise and taciturn.

MARY RUSSELL MITFORD (1787–1855) on Jane Austen

᠄᠉᠈᠉

I would venture to guess that Anon, who wrote so many
poems without signing them, was often a woman.

VIRGINIA WOOLF (1882–1941)

Even the Rose Has Thorns

On Women and Equality

Women have been called queens for a long time, but
the kingdom given them isn't worth ruling.

LOUISA MAY ALCOTT (1832–88)

No woman is all sweetness; even the rose has thorns.
JULIETTE RÉCAMIER (Jeanne Françoise Julie Adélaide Bernard,
Madame de Récamier, 1777–1849)

. . . women are the architects of society.

HARRIET BEECHER STOWE (1811–96)

A woman's hopes are woven of sunbeams; a shadow annihilates them.

GEORGE ELIOT (Mary Ann Evans, 1819–90)

᠄᠄᠄᠄

I think if women would indulge more freely in vituperation, they would enjoy ten times the health they do.

ELIZABETH CADY STANTON (1815–1902)

᠄᠄᠄᠄

One must choose between loving women and knowing them.

NINON (Anne) DE LENCLOS (1620–1705)

᠄᠄᠄᠄

It goes far towards reconciling me to being a woman when I reflect I am thus in no danger of marrying one.

LADY MARY WORTLEY MONTAGU (1689–1762)

᠄᠄᠄᠄

The great and almost only comfort about being a woman is that one can always pretend to be more stupid than one is and no one is surprised.

FREYA STARK (1893–1993)

᠄᠄᠄᠄

But what is woman? – only one of Nature's agreeable blunders.

HANNAH COWLEY (1743–1809)

There is no female mind. The brain is not an organ of
sex. As well speak of a female liver.

Charlotte Perkins Gilman (1860–1935)

჻᠗᠗჻

. . . spite will make a woman do more than love . . .

Margaret of Navarre (Marguerite d'Angoulême,
Queen of Navarre, 1492–1549)

჻᠗᠗჻

Many women, who have little or no sense of gratitude,
have a very quick one of jealousy.

Eliza Haywood (or Heywood, 1693–1756)

჻᠗᠗჻

Women are never stronger than when they arm
themselves with their weaknesses.

Marie-Anne, Marquise du Deffand (1697–1780)

჻᠗᠗჻

Being a woman has only bothered me in climbing trees.

Frances Perkins (1882–1965); she was the first woman
to be a member of a US presidential cabinet

჻᠗᠗჻

She wants to be perfect. That is her defect. . . . It is
vexatious that she is an angel. I had rather she were a
woman.

Marie-Anne, Marquise du Deffand (1697–1780)
on Madame de Choiseul

[86]

How much it is to be regretted, that the British ladies should ever sit down contented to polish, when they are able to reform; to entertain, when they might instruct; and to dazzle for an hour, when they are candidates for eternity!

HANNAH MORE (1745–1833)

〰️

I myself have never been able to find out precisely what feminism is: I only know that people call me a feminist whenever I express sentiments that differentiate me from a doormat or a prostitute.

REBECCA WEST (1892–1983)

〰️

The Queen is most anxious to enlist every one who can speak or write to join in checking this mad, wicked folly of 'Women's Rights', with all its attendant horrors, on which her poor feeble sex is bent, forgetting every sense of womanly feeling and propriety.

QUEEN VICTORIA (1819–1901),
in a letter to Sir Theodore Martin, 1870

I do not wish them to have power over men; but over
themselves.

Mary Wollstonecraft Godwin (1759–97)

❧❧❧

Woman, a pleasing but short-lived flower,
Too soft for business and too weak for power:
A wife in bondage, or neglected maid:
Despised if ugly; if she's fair, betrayed.

Mary Leapor (1722–46)

❧❧❧

The women who do the most work get the least money,
and the women who have the most money do the least
work.

Charlotte Perkins Gilman (1860–1935)

I ask no favours for my sex . . . All I ask
of our brethren is that they will take
their feet off from our necks.

SARAH MOORE GRIMKÉ (1792–1873)

⁓⁓⁓

Woman's discontent increases in
exact proportion to her development.

ELIZABETH CADY STANTON (1815–1902)

⁓⁓⁓

So long as women are slaves, men will
be knaves.

HELEN ROWLAND (1875–1950)

⁓⁓⁓

We hold these truths to be self-evident,
that all men and women are created
equal.

ELIZABETH CADY STANTON (1815–1902)

⁓⁓⁓

God would not give us the same talents if what were
right for men were wrong for women.

SARAH ORNE JEWETT (1849–1909)

⁓⁓⁓

Men of sense in all ages abhor those customs which
treat us only as the vassals of your sex.

ABIGAIL ADAMS (1744–1818)

Is it to be understood that the principles of the Declaration of Independence bear no relation to half of the human race?

HARRIET MARTINEAU (1802–76)

If women want any rights they had better take them and say nothing about it.

HARRIET BEECHER STOWE (1811–96)

Fireside occupation is one of the rights of women that men may envy.

HANNAH FARNHAM LEE (1780–1865)

I'm not surprised at what I've done.

MARGARET KNIGHT, a nineteenth-century inventor, especially of heavy machinery, responding to the inevitable remarks

Ladies were ladies in those days; they did not do things for themselves.

GWEN RAVERAT (1885–1957)

Virtue can only flourish amongst equals.

MARY WOLLSTONECRAFT GODWIN (1759–97)

Always Sure to Get Out of It

Men

No man is a hero to his valet.

Anne-Marie Bigot de Cornuel (1605–94)

꒜ꋮꋮ꒒

Mad, bad, and dangerous to know.

Lady Caroline Lamb (1785–1828)
on her former lover, Lord Byron

꒜ꋮꋮ꒒

. . . as for you men, you may, if you please, live and be slaves.

Boudicca (or Boadicea, *d.* AD 61), scornfully announcing
her resolve to resist the Romans, to conquer or die

꒜ꋮꋮ꒒

I require only three things in a man: he must be handsome, ruthless and stupid.

Dorothy Parker (1893–1967)

A man's mind, what there is of it, has always the
advantage of being masculine – as the smallest birch
tree is of a higher kind than the most soaring palm –
and even his ignorance is of a sounder quality.

GEORGE ELIOT (Mary Ann Evans, 1819–90)

If there is anything disagreeable going on men are
always sure to get out of it . . .

JANE AUSTEN (1775–1817)

Never trust a husband too far, nor a bachelor too near.

HELEN ROWLAND (1875–1950)

Gout is very much in my line, gentlemen are not.

ELIZABETH GARRETT ANDERSON (1836–1917)

Good morning, gentlemen both.

ELIZABETH I (1533–1603) greeting a group of 18 tailors

☙❧

Somehow a bachelor never quite gets over the idea that
he is a thing of beauty and a boy forever.

HELEN ROWLAND (1875–1950)

☙❧

A self-made man is one who believes in luck and sends
his son to Oxford.

CHRISTINA STEAD (1902–83), 1938

☙❧

There is no greater ninny than a man who thinks
himself cunning, nor any one wiser than he who knows
he is not so.

MARGARET OF NAVARRE (Marguerite d'Angoulême,
Queen of Navarre, 1492–1549)

☙❧

In men this blunder still you find
All think their little set mankind.

HANNAH MORE (1745–1833)

☙❧

There wouldn't be half as much fun in the world if it
weren't for children and men, and there ain't a mite of
difference between them under the skins.

ELLEN GLASGOW (1873–1945)

The more I see of men, the more I admire dogs.

Marie de Rabutin-Chantal, MADAME DE SÉVIGNÉ (1626–96)
(Also attributed to Jeanne-Marie, MADAME ROLAND [1754–93],
MADAME DE STAËL [1766–1817], and OUIDA [Louise Ramé
or de la Ramé, 1839–1908])

Why we oppose votes for men . . . because men are too
emotional to vote. Their conduct at baseball games and
political conventions shows this, while their innate
tendency to appeal to force renders them particularly
unfit for the task of government.

ALICE DUER MILLER (1874–1942)

The follies which a man regrets most in his life are those
which he didn't commit when he had the opportunity.

HELEN ROWLAND (1875–1950)

He is every other inch a gentleman.

REBECCA WEST (1892–1983)
of the novelist Michael Arlen

I fear nothing so much as a man who is witty all day long.

Marie de Rabutin-Chantal, MADAME DE SÉVIGNÉ
(1626–96)

ᔕᕆᕋᔆ

The way to a man's heart is through his stomach.

FANNY FERN (Sara Payson Parton, 1811–72)

ᔕᕆᕋᔆ

Adam's ready acquiescence with his wife's proposal, does not savor much of that superiority *in strength of mind*, which is arrogated by man.

SARAH MOORE GRIMKÉ (1792–1873)

God Made 'Em to
Match the Men

Men and Women

Why are women . . . so much more interesting to men than men are to women?

VIRGINIA WOOLF (1882–1941)

⚜

The hardest task in a girl's life is to prove to a man that his intentions are serious.

HELEN ROWLAND (1875–1950)

⚜

Man forgives woman anything save the wit to outwit him.

MINNA ANTRIM (1861–1950)

⚜

The usual masculine disillusionment in discovering that a woman has a brain.

MARGARET MITCHELL (1900–49)

⚜

Woman wants monogamy;
Man delights in novelty.

DOROTHY PARKER (1893–1967), 1927

⚜

Women have to be twice as good to get half as far as men.

AGNES MACPHAIL (1890–1954)

In passing, also, I'd like to say that the first time Adam had a chance he laid the blame on woman.

NANCY, LADY ASTOR (1879–1964)

🙘🙘

I'm not denyin' the women are foolish: God Almighty made 'em to match the men.

GEORGE ELIOT (Mary Ann Evans, 1819–90)

🙘🙘

Love is the whole history of a woman's life, it is but an episode in a man's.

Germaine Necker, MADAME DE STAËL (1766–1817)

🙘🙘

History tells me nothing that does not either vex or weary me; the men are all so good for nothing, and hardly any women at all.

JANE AUSTEN (1775–1817)

Women must come off the pedestal. Men put us up
there to get us out of the way.
                    VISCOUNTESS RHONDDA (1883–1958), 1920

꒰ೋ꒱

Stupid men, forever prone
To fix the blame on woman's reason,
When 'tis merely your own treason
That creates her fault alone!
                    JUANA INÉS DE LA CRUZ (1651–95)

꒰ೋ꒱

It is delightful to be a woman; but every man thanks the
Lord devoutly that he isn't one.
                    OLIVE SCHREINER (1855–1920)

꒰ೋ꒱

For just as women's bodies are softer than men's, so
their understanding is sharper.
                    CHRISTINE DE PISAN (c. 1363– c. 1430)

꒰ೋ꒱

. . . when women are the advisers, the lords of creation
don't take the advice till they have persuaded themselves that it is just what they intended to do; then they
act upon it, and if it succeeds, they give the weaker
vessel half the credit of it; if it fails, they generously give
her the whole.

                    LOUISA MAY ALCOTT (1832–88)

I love men, not because they are men, but because they are not women.

CHRISTINA, QUEEN OF SWEDEN (1626–89)

※※※

I will not say that women are better than men, but I will say that men are not so wise as I would wish them to be . . .

ESTER SOWERMAN (*fl.* 1617)

※※※

A good woman inspires a man; a brilliant woman interests him; a beautiful woman fascinates him; and a sympathetic woman gets him.

HELEN ROWLAND (1875–1950)

After the Hurly-Burly of the Chaise-Longue

Love and Matrimony

A woman despises a man for loving her unless she
returns his love.

ELIZABETH STODDARD (1823–1902)

ᗰᗩᗩᗰ

Four be the things I'd been better without:
Love, curiosity, freckles, and doubt.

DOROTHY PARKER (1893–1967), 1927

ᗰᗩᗩᗰ

She did observe, with some dismay, that far from
conquering all, love lazily sidestepped practical problems.

JEAN STAFFORD (1915–79)

ᗰᗩᗩᗰ

In matters of the heart nothing is true except the
improbable.

Germaine Necker, MADAME DE STAËL
(1766–1817)

ᗰᗩᗩᗰ

We don't believe in rheumatism and true love until after
the first attack.

MARIE VON EBNER-ESCHENBACH
(1830–1916)

ᗰᗩᗩᗰ

love is a very papithatick thing as well as troublesom and
tiresome . . .

MARJORY FLEMING (1803–11)

Nothing to be done without a bribe I find, in love as well as law.

SUSANNAH CENTLIVRE (*c.* 1669–1723)

☙❧

Love never dies of starvation, but often of indigestion.

NINON (Anne) DE LENCLOS (1620–1705)

☙❧

If only one could tell true love from false love as one can tell mushrooms from toadstools.

KATHERINE MANSFIELD (1888–1923)

☙❧

Now love the limb-loosener sweeps me away . . .

SAPPHO (7th–6th century BC)

Remember my unalterable maxim, 'When we love we
always have something to say.'

LADY MARY WORTLEY MONTAGU (1689–1762)

॰ঽৎ৶

We cannot really love anybody with whom we never
laugh.

AGNES REPPLIER (1858–1950)

॰ঽৎ৶

Tears may be dried up, but the heart – never.

MARGUERITE DE VALOIS (1553–1615)

॰ঽৎ৶

[Nothing] . . . leads to love. It is love who throws himself
across your path. And then he either blocks it for ever
or, if he abandons it, leaves it in rack and ruin.

(Sidonie-Gabrielle) COLETTE (1873–1954)

॰ঽৎ৶

'Tis not love's going that hurts my days,
but that it went in little ways.

EDNA ST VINCENT MILLAY (1892–1950)

॰ঽৎ৶

When a girl marries, she exchanges the attentions of
many men for the inattention of one.

HELEN ROWLAND (1875–1950)

I married beneath me. All women do.

NANCY, LADY ASTOR (1879–1964)

⁘

A positive engagement to marry a certain person at a certain time, at all haps and hazards, I have always considered the most ridiculous thing on earth.

JANE WELSH CARLYLE (1801–66)

⁘

Any intelligent woman who reads the marriage contract, and then goes into it, deserves all the consequences.

ISADORA DUNCAN (1878–1927)

⁘

Marriage is the result of the longing for the deep, deep peace of the double bed after the hurly-burly of the chaise-longue.

MRS PATRICK (Beatrice Stella) CAMPBELL (1865–1940)

A lady's imagination is very rapid; it jumps from admiration to love, from love to matrimony in a moment.

JANE AUSTEN (1775–1817)

ᔐᖇᖇᓑ

Happiness in marriage is entirely a matter of chance.

JANE AUSTEN (1775–1817)

ᔐᖇᖇᓑ

Marriage is a lottery in which men stake their liberty and women their happiness.

RENÉE DE CHATEAUNEUF-RIEUX (1550–87)

ᔐᖇᖇᓑ

So that ends my first experience with matrimony, which I always thought a highly overrated performance.

ISADORA DUNCAN (1878–1927)

ᔐᖇᖇᓑ

When you see what some girls marry, you realize how they must hate to work for a living.

HELEN ROWLAND (1875–1950)

ᔐᖇᖇᓑ

I have very little of Mr Blake's company. He is always in paradise.

CATHERINE BLAKE, of her husband, William
(1757–1827)

Girls! Girls! . . . never develop a reputation for being clever. It will put you out of the matrimonial running as effectually as though it had been circulated that you had leprosy.

(Stella Maria Sarah) MILES FRANKLIN
(1879–1954)

Single women have a dreadful propensity for being poor – which is one very strong argument in favour of matrimony.

JANE AUSTEN (1775–1817)

⁵ℛℛℭ

That is partly why women marry – to keep up the fiction of being in the hub of things.

ELIZABETH BOWEN (1899–1973), 1935

⁵ℛℛℭ

Marriage, to women as to men, must be a luxury, not a necessity; an incident of life, not all of it.

SUSAN BROWNELL ANTHONY (1820–1906)

A husband is what is left of a lover, after the nerve has been extracted.

HELEN ROWLAND (1875–1950)

꒰ꂦꀦꂦ꒱

The people people have for friends
Your common sense appall,
But the people people marry
Are the queerest folk of all.

CHARLOTTE PERKINS GILMAN
(1860–1935)

꒰ꂦꀦꂦ꒱

No divorcees were included, except those who had shown signs of penitence by being remarried to the very wealthy.

EDITH WHARTON (1862–1937)

In a successful marriage there is no such thing as one's way. There is only the way of both, only the bumpy, dusty, difficult, but always mutual path!

PHYLLIS MCGINLEY (1905–78)

ℭ℧℧ℭ

Marriage is the grave or tomb of wit.

MARGARET CAVENDISH, DUCHESS OF NEWCASTLE
(c. 1624– c.74)

ℭ℧℧ℭ

A woman, let her be as good as she may, has got to put up with the life her husband makes for her.

GEORGE ELIOT (Mary Ann Evans, 1819–90)

ℭ℧℧ℭ

It is always incomprehensible to a man that a woman should ever refuse an offer of marriage.

JANE AUSTEN (1775–1817); she herself refused offers
of marriage, and on one occasion, having actually accepted,
changed her mind the following morning

ℭ℧℧ℭ

If you cannot have your dear husband for a comfort and a delight, for a breadwinner and a crosspatch, for a sofa, a chair or a hot-water bottle, one can use him as a Cross to be Borne.

STEVIE SMITH (1902–71), 1936

. . . my husbands have been very unlucky.

LUCREZIA BORGIA (1480–1519),
after the murder of her second husband

᠔᠙᠙᠑

Indeed he has all the qualities that would make a
husband tolerable – battlement, veranda, stable, etc., no
grins and no glass in his eye.

GEORGE ELIOT (Mary Ann Evans, 1819–90)

᠔᠙᠙᠑

It is a truth universally acknowledged, that a single man
in possession of a good fortune, must be in want of a
wife.

JANE AUSTEN (1775–1817)

᠔᠙᠙᠑

Ask half the married women in the nation how they
became wives: they will tell you their friends urged
them.

FANNY BURNEY (Frances, Madame d'Arblay, 1752–1840)

᠔᠙᠙᠑

A real marriage bears no resemblance to these
marriages of interest or ambition. It is two lovers who
live together.

LADY MARY WORTLEY MONTAGU (1689–1762)

Now at least I know where he is.
QUEEN ALEXANDRA (1844–1925),
after the death of her husband, Edward VII, in 1910

᠖᠙᠙᠖

Having once embarked on your marital voyage, it is impossible not to be aware that you make no way and that the sea is not within sight – that, in fact, you are exploring an enclosed basin.
GEORGE ELIOT (Mary Ann Evans, 1819–90)

᠖᠙᠙᠖

Marriage: a souvenir of love.
HELEN ROWLAND (1875–1950)

᠖᠙᠙᠖

My own, or other people's?
PEGGY GUGGENHEIM (1898–1975), in answer to the question
'How many husbands have you had?'

᠖᠙᠙᠖

I would rather be a beggar and single, than a Queen and married . . . I should call the wedding ring the yoke ring.
ELIZABETH I (1533–1603)

The state of matrimony is a dangerous disease: far better to take drink in my opinion.

Marie de Rabutin-Chantal, MADAME DE SÉVIGNÉ
(1626–96)

ꙅ୧୧ꙅ

... a state that causes the misery of three quarters of the human race.

Françoise d'Aubigné, MADAME DE MAINTENON
(1635–1719)

ꙅ୧୧ꙅ

Dear, never forget one little point: it's my business, you just work here.

ELIZABETH ARDEN (c. 1880–1966)
to her husband, manager of her company

I Am Wiser
to Know

Friends and
Enemies

Four be the things I am wiser to know:
Idleness, sorrow, a friend, and a foe.

DOROTHY PARKER (1893–1967), 1937

☽☾☽☾

I always felt that the great high privilege, relief and comfort of friendship was that one had to explain nothing.

KATHERINE MANSFIELD (1888–1923)

☽☾☽☾

'Stay' is a charming word in a friend's vocabulary.

LOUISA MAY ALCOTT (1832–88)

☽☾☽☾

The heart may think it knows better: the senses know that absence blots people out. We have really no absent friends.

ELIZABETH BOWEN (1899–1973), 1938

☽☾☽☾

Animals are such agreeable friends – they ask no questions, they pass no criticisms.

GEORGE ELIOT (Mary Ann Evans, 1819–90)

☽☾☽☾

Friends can see defects with the naked eye, however weak that organ may be; but too frequently require magnifying glasses to discover good qualities.

MARGUERITE, LADY BLESSINGTON (1789–1849)

Every murderer is probably somebody's old friend.
AGATHA CHRISTIE (1890–1976), 1920

Life becomes useless and insipid when we have no longer either friends or enemies.
CHRISTINA, QUEEN OF SWEDEN (1626–89)

Intimacies between women often go backwards, beginning in revelations and ending up in small talk, without loss of esteem.
ELIZABETH BOWEN (1899–1973), 1938

People wish their enemies dead – but I do not; I say give them the gout, give them the stone!

Lady Mary Wortley Montagu (1689–1762)

❧❦❦❧

I have lost friends, some by death . . . others through sheer inability to cross the street.

Virginia Woolf (1882–1941)

❧❦❦❧

There are times when one cannot lift a blade of grass without finding a serpent underneath it.

Marceline Desbordes-Valmore (1786–1859)

❧❦❦❧

Yes'm, old friends is always best, 'less you can catch a new one that's fit to make an old one out of.

Sarah Orne Jewett (1849–1909)

❧❦❦❧

True friendship is never serene.

Marie de Rabutin-Chantal, Madame de Sévigné (1626–96)

❧❦❦❧

Treat your friends as you do your pictures, and place them in their best light.

Lady Randolph Churchill (née Jennie Jerome, 1854–1921)

Business, you know, may bring money, but friendship
hardly ever does.

JANE AUSTEN (1775–1817)

꒰ꔷꔷ꒱

My true friends have always given me that supreme
proof of devotion, a spontaneous aversion to the man I
loved.

(Sidonie-Gabrielle) COLETTE, (1873–1954)

꒰ꔷꔷ꒱

Friendships begin with liking or gratitude – roots that
can be pulled up.

GEORGE ELIOT (Mary Ann Evans, 1819–90)

To have a good enemy, choose a friend; he knows where
to strike.

Diane de Poitiers (1499–1566)

૩൨൨ඌ

God gave us our relatives; thank God we can choose our
friends.

Ethel Watts Mumford (1878–1940)

૩൨൨ඌ

That Dear Octopus

The Family

For it is impossible for a man to put forward fair and honest views about our affairs if he has not, like everyone else, children whose lives may be at stake.

ASPASIA (*fl. c.* 440–420 BC),
speech written for Pericles, *c.* 431

꒰ꪀꪀ꒱

The best way to keep children home is to make the home atmosphere pleasant and let the air out of the tires.

DOROTHY PARKER (1893–1967)

꒰ꪀꪀ꒱

. . . for the sins of children rise up in judgement against their parents.

LADY CAROLINE LAMB (1785–1828)

It is not a bad thing that children should occasionally,
and politely, put parents in their place.

(Sidonie-Gabrielle) COLETTE (1873–1954)

ↄ℞℞ↄ

Most mothers think that to keep young people away
from love-making it is enough never to speak of it in
their presence.

MARIE-MADELEINE DE LA FAYETTE (1634–93)

ↄ℞℞ↄ

Politeness, that cementer of friendship and soother of
enmities, is nowhere so much required, and so frequently
outraged, as in family circles.

MARGUERITE, LADY BLESSINGTON (1789–1849)

Childhood is never troubled with foresight.

FANNY BURNEY (Frances, Madame d'Arblay, 1752–1840)

꒰ꕤꕥꕥꕤ꒱

. . . children servants master father mother, things that though they are blessings yet often they prove otherwise, and the best of them have days in which one thinks one could live without them.

MARGARET GODOLPHIN (1652–78)

꒰ꕤꕥꕥꕤ꒱

The family – that dear octopus from whose tentacles we never quite escape.

DODIE SMITH (1896–1990), 1938

Not the Person
I Took Me For

The Self

I know they are most deceived that trusteth most in themselves.

ELIZABETH I (1533–1603)

⸙⸙⸙

You grow up the day you have your first real laugh at yourself.

ETHEL BARRYMORE (1879–1959)

⸙⸙⸙

I have often wished I had time to cultivate modesty . . . but I am too busy thinking about myself.

EDITH SITWELL (1887–1964), 1950

⸙⸙⸙

. . . I'm not going to lie down and let trouble walk over me.

ELLEN GLASGOW (1873–1945)

⸙⸙⸙

There are some secrets which scarcely admit of being disclosed even to ourselves.

JANE WEST (1758–1852)

⸙⸙⸙

My vigour, vitality and cheek repel me. I am the kind of woman I would run away from.

NANCY, LADY ASTOR (1879–1964)

I am never afraid of what I know.

ANNA SEWELL (1820–78)

❧

For whomsoever I do good they harm me most.

SAPPHO (7th–6th century BC)

❧

How prone we are to blame others, when we ourselves only are in fault.

MARGUERITE, LADY BLESSINGTON (1789–1849)

❧

The Jews have produced only three originative geniuses: Christ, Spinoza, and myself.

GERTRUDE STEIN (1874–1946)

❧

Real education should educate us out of self into something far finer; into a selflessness which links us with all humanity.

NANCY, LADY ASTOR (1879–1964)

I have a gift for enraging people, but if I ever bore you,
it will be with a knife.

LOUISE BROOKS (1906–85)

᪥᪥᪥

I am not at all the sort of person you and I took me for.

JANE WELSH CARLYLE (1801–66)

᪥᪥᪥

'Know thyself' is a most superfluous direction. We can't
avoid it. We can only hope that no one else knows.

IVY COMPTON-BURNETT (1884–1969), 1939

᪥᪥᪥

To have the courage of your excess – to find the limit of
yourself.

KATHERINE MANSFIELD (1888–1923)

᪥᪥᪥

I can see that the Lady has a genius for ruling, whilst I
have a genius for not being ruled.

JANE WELSH CARLYLE (1801–66)

᪥᪥᪥

I give myself sometimes admirable advice, but am
incapable of taking it.

LADY MARY WORTLEY MONTAGU (1689–1762)

. . . everything seems insupportable to me. This may
very well be because I am insupportable myself.

MARIE-ANNE, MARQUISE DU DEFFAND (1697–1780)

᠙᠗᠙᠗

I am one of the people who love the why of things.

CATHERINE THE GREAT, Empress of Russia (1729–96)

᠙᠗᠙᠗

Whenever I dwell for any length of time on my own
shortcomings, they gradually begin to seem mild,
harmless, rather engaging little things, not at all like the
staring defects in other people's characters.

MARGARET HALSEY (1910–97), 1938

᠙᠗᠙᠗

It is never too late to be what you might have been.

GEORGE ELIOT (Mary Ann Evans, 1819–90)

People Are Only Human

Human Nature

Well, of course, people are only human . . . But it does not seem much for them to be.

IVY COMPTON-BURNETT (1884–1969), 1939

ᔦᔨᔩᔪ

If only we'd stop trying to be happy, we could have a pretty good time.

EDITH WHARTON (1862–1937)

ᔦᔨᔩᔪ

Curious things, habits. People themselves never knew they had them.

AGATHA CHRISTIE (1890–1976), 1924

ᔦᔨᔩᔪ

We are so vain that we even care for the opinion of those we don't care for.

MARIE VON EBNER-ESCHENBACH (1830–1916)

ᔦᔨᔩᔪ

People are always willing to follow advice when it accords with their own wishes . . .

MARGUERITE, LADY BLESSINGTON (1789–1849)

ᔦᔨᔩᔪ

It is vain to say human beings ought to be satisfied with tranquillity: they must have action; and they will make it if they cannot find it.

GEORGE ELIOT (Mary Ann Evans, 1819–90)

Science may have found a cure for most evils; but it has found no remedy for the worst of them all – the apathy of human beings.

HELEN KELLER (1880–1968)

᠕ᘉᘉᘈ

There are only two distinct classes of people on this earth: those who espouse enthusiasm and those who despise it.

Germaine Necker, MADAME DE STAËL
(1766–1817)

᠕ᘉᘉᘈ

Some people are moulded by their admirations, others by their hostilities.

ELIZABETH BOWEN (1899–1973), 1938

᠕ᘉᘉᘈ

It is natural to avoid those to whom we have been too much obliged . . . uncommon generosity causes neglect rather than ingratitude.

HÉLOÏSE (c. 1098–1164)

᠕ᘉᘉᘈ

Someone has somewhere commented on the fact that millions long for immortality who don't know what to do with themselves on a rainy Sunday afternoon.

SUSAN ERTZ (1894–1985), 1943

I enjoy vast delight in the folly of mankind; and, God be praised, that is an inexhaustible source of entertainment.

LADY MARY WORTLEY MONTAGU (1689–1762)

❧☙

'Tis easy enough to be pleasant
When life flows along like a song;
But the man worth while is the one who will smile
When everything goes dead wrong.

ELLA WHEELER WILCOX (1855–1919)

❧☙

. . . people who do not get into scrapes are a great deal less interesting than those who do.

MURASAKI SHIKIBU (974–?1031)

❧☙

One half of the world cannot understand the pleasures of the other.

JANE AUSTEN (1775–1817)

❧☙

The human heart has hidden treasures,
In secret held, in silence sealed.

CHARLOTTE BRONTË (1816–55)

A Progress
in Spirals

Wisdom
and Learning

The human mind always makes progress, but it is a
progress in spirals.

Germaine Necker, MADAME DE STAËL (1766–1817)

❦❧❦

Genius is the gold in the mine; talent is the miner that
works and brings it out.

MARGUERITE, LADY BLESSINGTON (1789–1849)

❦❧❦

It takes a lot of time to be a genius, you have to sit
around so much doing nothing, really doing nothing.

GERTRUDE STEIN (1874–1946)

❦❧❦

No one can arrive from being talented alone. God gives
talent, work transforms talent into genius.

ANNA PAVLOVA (1881–1931)

❦❧❦

Genius, whether locked up in a cell or roaming at large,
is always solitary.

GEORGE SAND (Amandine-Aurore Lucille Dupin,
Baronne Dudevant,1804–76)

❦❧❦

The majority of minds are no more to be controlled by
strong reason than plum-pudding is to be grasped by
sharp pincers.

GEORGE ELIOT (Mary Ann Evans, 1819–90)

True knowledge consists in knowing things not words.

LADY MARY WORTLEY MONTAGU (1689–1762)

*

It is not depravity that afflicts the human race so much as a general lack of intelligence.

AGNES REPPLIER (1858–1950)

*

Since when was genius found respectable?

ELIZABETH BARRETT BROWNING (1806–61)

*

Most beautiful dumb girls think they are smart and get away with it, because other people, on the whole, aren't much smarter.

LOUISE BROOKS (1906–85)

Too much rigidity on the part of teachers should be followed by a brisk spirit of insubordination on the part of the taught.

AGNES REPPLIER (1858–1950)

ᘓᗡᗡᘒ

Brass shines as fair to the ignorant as gold to the gold-smith.

ELIZABETH I (1533–1603)

ᘓᗡᗡᘒ

Teach him to think for himself? Oh, my God, teach him rather to think like other people!

MARY SHELLEY (1797–1851) on her son's education

ᘓᗡᗡᘒ

Yet if thou didst but know how little wit governs this mighty universe.

APHRA BEHN (1640–89)

ᘓᗡᗡᘒ

People are never so near playing the fool as when they think themselves wise.

LADY MARY WORTLEY MONTAGU (1689–1762)

ᘓᗡᗡᘒ

All our talents increase in the using, and every faculty, both good and bad, strengthens by exercise.

ANNE BRONTË (1820–49)

Prejudices, it is well known, are most difficult to eradicate from the heart whose soil has never been loosened or fertilized by education; they grow there, firm as weeds among rocks.

CHARLOTTE BRONTË (1816–55)

⧓

Better build schoolrooms for the boy,
Than cells and gibbets for the man.

ELIZA COOK (1818–89)

⧓

Science may carry us to Mars, but it will leave the earth peopled as ever by the inept.

AGNES REPPLIER (1858–1950)

⧓

It takes people a long time to learn the difference between talent and genius, especially ambitious young men and women.

LOUISA MAY ALCOTT (1832–88)

One Damn Thing
Over and Over

Life

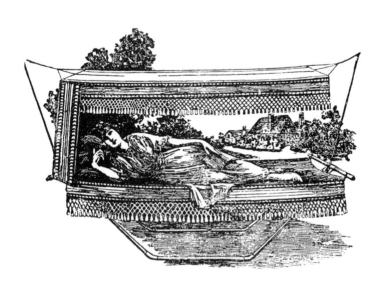

Life is either always a tightrope or a feather bed. Give
me the tightrope.

EDITH WHARTON (1862–1937)

5∂∂C

It is not true that life is one damn thing after another –
it's one damn thing over and over.

EDNA ST VINCENT MILLAY (1892–1950)

5∂∂C

Life appears to me too short to be spent in nursing
animosity or registering wrong.

CHARLOTTE BRONTË (1816–55)

5∂∂C

What I love about noise is that it camouflages life.

Germaine Necker, MADAME DE STAËL
(1766–1817)

5∂∂C

Sooner or later we all discover that the important
moments in life are not the advertised ones, not the
birthdays, the graduations, the weddings, not the great
goals achieved. The real milestones are less prepossess-
ing. They come to the door of memory unannounced,
stray dogs that amble in, sniff round a bit, and simply
never leave. Our lives are measured by these.

SUSAN BROWNELL ANTHONY (1820–1906)

I have learned to live each day as it comes, and not to
borrow trouble by dreading tomorrow. It is the dark
menace of the future that makes cowards of us all.

DOROTHY DIX (1870–1951)

უ૨૨Ც

The surest way to get a thing in this life is to be prepared
for doing without it, to the exclusion even of hope.

JANE WELSH CARLYLE (1801–66)

უ૨૨Ც

As soon as life becomes bearable we stop analysing it . . .
A tranquil day is spoiled by being examined.

GEORGE SAND (Amandine-Aurore Lucille Dupin,
Baronne Dudevant, 1804–76)

Courage is the price that life exacts for granting peace.

AMELIA EARHART (1898–1937)

❧ ❧ ❧

Life is so constructed, that the event does not, cannot, will not match the expectation.

CHARLOTTE BRONTË (1816–55)

❧ ❧ ❧

Nothing in life is to be feared. It is only to be understood.

MARIE CURIE (1867–1934)

❧ ❧ ❧

I slept, and dreamed that life was beauty
I woke – and found that life was duty.

ELLEN STURGIS HOOPER (1816–41)

❧ ❧ ❧

Life was meant to be lived, and curiosity must be kept alive. One must never, for whatever reason, turn his back on life.

ELEANOR ROOSEVELT (1884–1962)

❧ ❧ ❧

To live is so startling it leaves little time for anything else.

EMILY DICKINSON (1830–86)

Of No Use
to an Emperor

Philosophy

No idea is so antiquated that it was not once modern. No idea is so modern that it will not some day be antiquated.

ELLEN GLASGOW (1873–1945)

꒰ꃞꃞ꒱

My definition is of a man up in a balloon, with his family and friends holding the ropes which confine him to the earth and trying to haul him down.

LOUISA MAY ALCOTT (1832–88)
on how she sees a philosopher

꒰ꃞꃞ꒱

One way of getting an idea of our fellow-countrymen's miseries is to go and look at their pleasures.

GEORGE ELIOT (Mary Ann Evans, 1819–90)

꒰ꃞꃞ꒱

He who influences the thought of his times, influences all the times that follow. He has made his impress on eternity.

HYPATIA (c. 370–415)

꒰ꃞꃞ꒱

No philosophy, my son: it is of no use to an emperor.

AGRIPPINA THE YOUNGER (AD15–59),
advice to Nero

A fool bolts pleasure, then complains of moral indigestion.

MINNA ANTRIM (1861–1950)

ॐௐௐॐ

Nothing is so good as it seems beforehand.

GEORGE ELIOT (Mary Ann Evans, 1819–90)

ॐௐௐॐ

A vacuum can only exist, I imagine, by the things that enclose it.

ZELDA FITZGERALD (1900–48)

ॐௐௐॐ

There is always a 'but' in this imperfect world.

ANNE BRONTË (1820–49)

ॐௐௐॐ

It behoved that there should be sin; but all shall be well, and all shall be well, and all manner of thing shall be well.

JULIAN OF NORWICH (*c.* 1342– *c.* 1429)

ॐௐௐॐ

When one door of happiness closes, another opens; but often we look so long at the closed door that we do not see the one which has been opened for us.

HELEN KELLER (1880–1968)

They who see only what they wish to see in those around them are very fortunate.

MARIE BASHKIRTSEFF (1860–84)

꒰ঌ৶ৎ꒱

We cannot take anything for granted, beyond the first mathematical formula. Question everything else.

MARIA MITCHELL (1818–89)

꒰ঌ৶ৎ꒱

All sins are attempts to fill voids.

SIMONE WEIL (1909–43)

꒰ঌ৶ৎ꒱

There are two ways of spreading light: to be the candle, or the mirror that reflects it.

EDITH WHARTON (1862–1937)

꒰ঌ৶ৎ꒱

No man chooses evil because it is evil; he only mistakes it for happiness, the good he seeks.

MARY WOLLSTONECRAFT GODWIN
(1759–97)

꒰ঌ৶ৎ꒱

Experience is a good teacher, but she sends in terrific bills.

MINNA ANTRIM (1861–1950)

I avoid looking forward or backward, and try to keep looking upward.

CHARLOTTE BRONTË (1816–55)

🙰🙰🙰

Considering how dangerous everything is nothing is frightening.

GERTRUDE STEIN (1874–1946)

🙰🙰🙰

So this gentleman said a girl with brains ought to do something with them besides think.

ANITA LOOS (1893–1981), 1925

🙰🙰🙰

I make the most of all that comes, and the least of all that goes.

SARA TEASDALE (1884–1933)

Why not seize the pleasure at once? How often is happiness destroyed by preparation, foolish preparation!

JANE AUSTEN (1775–1817)

🥢

Saddle your dreams afore you ride 'em.

MARY WEBB (1881–1927)

🥢

Time, that omnipotent effacer of eternal passions . . .

MARGUERITE, LADY BLESSINGTON (1789–1849)

It is sometimes best to slide over thoughts and not go to the bottom of them.

Marie de Rabutin-Chantal, MADAME DE SÉVIGNÉ (1626–96)

❧

Avoiding danger is no safer in the long run than outright exposure. The fearful are caught as often as the bold.

HELEN KELLER (1880–1968)

❧

When one has been threatened with a great injustice, one accepts a smaller as a favour.

JANE WELSH CARLYLE (1801–66)

❧

No good deed goes unpunished.

CLARE BOOTHE LUCE (1903–87)

❧

The beauty of the world, which is so soon to perish, has two edges, one of laughter, one of anguish, cutting the heart asunder.

VIRGINIA WOOLF (1882–1941)

Except Taxes

On Death
and Last Words

While we are young the idea of death or failure is
intolerable to us; even the possibility of ridicule we
cannot bear.

ISAK DINESEN (Karen Blixen, 1885–1962), 1934

I have a horror of death; the dead are so soon
forgotten. But when I die, they'll have to remember me.

EMILY DICKINSON (1830–86)

Razors pain you;
Rivers are damp;
Acids stain you;
And drugs cause cramp.
Guns aren't lawful;
Nooses give;
Gas smells awful;
You might as well live.

DOROTHY PARKER
(1893–1967), 1937

I know some poison I could drink;
I've often thought I'd taste it;
But Mother bought it for the sink
And drinking it would waste it.

EDNA ST VINCENT MILLAY
(1892–1950)

There's something dreadfully decisive about a beheading.

AGNES SMEDLEY (?1894–1950)

🙛🐱🙙

My dear – the people we should have been seen dead with.

REBECCA WEST (1892–1983), telegram to Noël Coward on learning that they had both been on the Nazi black list

🙛🐱🙙

Death and taxes and childbirth! There's never any convenient time for any of them.

MARGARET MITCHELL (1900–49)

We met . . . Dr Hall in such very deep mourning that either his mother, his wife or himself must be dead.

JANE AUSTEN (1775–1817)

〰〰〰

Matter and death are mortal illusions.

MARY BAKER EDDY (1821–1910),
herself now presumably a mortal illusion

〰〰〰

Childhood is the kingdom where nobody dies.

EDNA ST VINCENT MILLAY (1892–1950)

〰〰〰

If you will send for a doctor I will see him now.

EMILY BRONTË (1818–48)

〰〰〰

Monsieur, I beg your pardon. I did not do it on purpose.

MARIE-ANTOINETTE, Queen Consort of France (Josèphe
Jeanne Marie-Antoinette, 1755–93), as she stumbled over the
executioner's foot on the way to the guillotine

〰〰〰

Let me go! Let me go!

CLARA BARTON (1821–1912)

Take courage, Charlotte, take courage!
ANNE BRONTË (1820–49)

ɔ☊☊ɔ

How imperious one is when one no longer has the time
to be polite.
JEANNE-LOUISE-HENRIETTE CAMPAN (1752–1822),
who had just issued an order to a servant

Beautiful.

ELIZABETH BARRETT BROWNING (1806–61),
when asked how she was feeling

Ah, my God, I am dead!

CATHERINE DE MÉDICIS,
Queen Consort of France (1519–89),
slightly anticipating events

Nothing but death.

JANE AUSTEN (1775–1817), when asked what she required

What is the answer? [No reply. Laughs.] In that case what is the question?

GERTRUDE STEIN (1874–1946)

They have made me tipsy. Stocky! Stocky!

CHARLOTTE AUGUSTA, PRINCESS OF WALES
(1796–1817), calling for Baron Stockmar,
the court physician (she died in childbirth)

Yes, it is indeed frightful weather for a journey as long as the one before me.

MARIE-THÉRÈSE OF AUSTRIA,
Queen Consort of France (1638–83)

Oh that peace may come. Bertie!

> QUEEN VICTORIA (1819–1901),
> who had been waiting to see her beloved Albert

꒰ঌ৩ঌ꒱

That will be nice.

> MARY WEBB (1881–1927), told that everyone
> would gather for tea that afternoon

꒰ঌ৩ঌ꒱

Go first. At least I can spare you the pain of seeing my blood flow.

> Jeanne-Marie, MADAME ROLAND (1754–93),
> herself a revolutionary, to a frightened old man,
> both about to be guillotined by the Jacobins

꒰ঌ৩ঌ꒱

I'm going to Dr Caldwell's for one of my regular treatments.

> JEANNE EAGELS (d. 1929)

Today I am better, but if you wish for another cheerful evening with your old friend, there is no time to be lost.

MARY RUSSELL MITFORD (1787–1855)

༄རྒྱ

I see no reason why the existence of Harriet Martineau should be perpetuated.

HARRIET MARTINEAU (1802–76)

༄རྒྱ

Get my Swan costume ready.

ANNA PAVLOVA (1881–1931)

༄རྒྱ

It has all been very interesting.

LADY MARY WORTLEY MONTAGU (1689–1762)

༄རྒྱ

Is it not meningitis?

LOUISA MAY ALCOTT (1832–88)

༄རྒྱ

Except taxes.

ELISA BONAPARTE (1777–1820),
sister of Napoleon (concluding the remark
'Nothing is as certain as death . . .')